As of Nov 08, 2023

4,347.35

13.23%
YTD RETURN

The index Launch Date is Mar 04, 1957. All information for an index prior to its Launch Date is hypothetical back-tested, not actual performance, based on the index methodology in effect on the Launch Date. SEE MORE ⌄

Important Disclosures

We are not investment advisors or investment planners, we are financial educators, insurance agents, case designers, our solutions are an alternative to the products that advisors recommend. Our clients bank like a bank. We are not fishing for you, not charging you for the fish, not charging you for catching the fish, or charging you for telling you where the fish are. We are teaching you how to fish for yourself.

Our strategy includes technology that offers algorithm driven debt elimination & interest cancelation. The solution includes life insurance & annuities that offer indexing, no fees, no caps, no surrender charges, unlimited compound interest returns for life, no risk of principal, an estate, life & death protection, wealth building, tax advantages on returns, tax advantages for existing retirement accounts, IRS code benefits, no recourse, borrowing money from yourself, while earning interest on your loans, the ability to bank the way banks do and turn liabilities into income.

Hypothetical or model performance results have certain limitations including, but not limited to: hypothetical results do not take into account actual trading and market factors (such as liquidity disruptions, etc.). Simulated performance assumes frictionless transaction costs and no lag between signal generation and implementation. Simulated performance is designed with the benefit of hindsight and there can be no assurance that the strategy presented would have been able to achieve the results shown. There are frequently large differences between hypothetical performance results and actual results from any investment strategy. While data was obtained from sources believed to be reliable, mainly Artificial Intelligence, Financial Literacy Group, LLC ("FLG") and its affiliates provide no assurances as to its accuracy or completeness.

This material has been provided for informational purposes only and should not be construed as investment advice or an offer, solicitation or recommendation to buy, sell or hold any particular investment product, strategy, investment manager or account arrangement, and should not serve as a primary basis for investment decisions. Prospective investors should consult a legal, tax or financial professional in order to determine whether any investment product, strategy or service is appropriate for their particular circumstances. This material may not be used for the purpose of an offer or solicitation in any jurisdiction or in any circumstances in which such offer or solicitation is unlawful or not authorized. Some information contained herein has been obtained from third party sources that are believed to be reliable, but the information has not been independently verified. No part of this material may be reproduced in any form, or referred to in any other publication, without express written permission.

Indices referred to herein are used for comparative and informational purposes only and have been selected because they are generally considered to be representative of certain markets. Comparisons to indices as benchmarks have limitations because indices have volatility and other material characteristics that may differ from the portfolio, investment or hedge to which they are compared.

The Standard & Poor's 500 (S&P 500) Index is a widely accepted, unmanaged index of US stock market performance. Investors cannot invest directly in an index.

Forward

Banking Solutions and Why Hybrid Arbitrage? Just a few short years ago in 2019, I was staunchly opposed to indexed universal life insurance, because that's what I was taught by the national "banks" and "gurus" years ago. I believed (as many people still do) that if you need life insurance, you should buy a term policy, then take the difference in premiums between whole life and term and invest it in mutual funds.

Advisors also say that you shouldn't pay off your house early because a home loan is cheap money and you can't get to your equity. That money can be used for investing, as if you will never lose money in the market and as if advisors don't make points whether you make money or not.

So when a friend of mine sat me down and tried to show me how I could bank like the banks do, I nearly refused to listen. Many of you reading this will feel the same way, and nothing I say will change your minds. That's fine, you're entitled to your opinion just as I was entitled to mine.

Thankfully, my associate showed me how a properly designed indexed universal life insurance policy and hybrid financial arbitrage works. I soon realized that the gurus and advisors of today were correct, based on the information they'd been given. The problem was their information was incomplete and that's why hybrid financial arbitrage was outside their realm of thinking.

We are providing a comprehensive overview of a financial strategy aimed at achieving debt freedom, reducing interest by up to 75%, getting to equity in 5 -7 years, not paying the bank this money and earning the interest on your own loans.

This includes financial literacy, and wealth creation through the use of advanced financial products like Indexed Universal Life (IUL) insurance and annuities. This plan proposes a series of steps that guide individuals from understanding their current financial position through various stages such as managing cash flow, reducing debt, combining IULs and annuities, building a real estate portfolio, ultimately securing lifelong retirement income and generational wealth.

The strategy includes educational components like financial literacy courses, practical tools such as bookkeeping software for tracking finances, and sophisticated techniques like using IUL policies for banking purposes to leverage liabilities into assets. The report suggests that by borrowing against an IUL policy, one can effectively "pay themselves" the interest rather than financial institutions, thus retaining more wealth within one's personal economy.

Moreover, the plan highlights the importance of creating a solid estate plan, utilizing tax-advantaged vehicles for saving for children's education, and developing a savvy asset strategy that includes real estate equity. The roadmap also emphasizes the use of technology and AI to accelerate debt repayment and reduce interest payments.

For retirement, the strategy encourages the use of indexed annuities to protect principal and ensure a steady income stream for life. It details how rollovers from traditional retirement accounts into these annuities can be optimized to maximize wealth and minimize tax implications, with the use of the IUL policy to manage and grow the withdrawn funds.

Hybrid Arbitrage, a solution that is a unique combination of GPS debt technology (No refinance, modification, settlement or consolidation) and a special kind of no surrender charge, no cap, no fee index universal life insurance, POLI (Private Owned Life Insurance), the kind that banks use. This type of BOLI can be used by any American adult, family and business owner. Hybrid Arbitrage turns Infinite Banking, BYOB, Velocity Banking or any other type of banking solution previously used, on its head. This has never been done before.

Overall, this Hybrid Arbitrage Retirement Solution can be used by any middle class person even with a minimum of discretionary income. Throughout this e-Book we look at what your retirement will look like and we highlight the differences in what we do versus the advisors who cater to the wealthy population.

This guide aims to educate and empower normal working class individuals to take control of their financial future, reduce reliance on traditional banking and lending institutions, and create a self-sustaining financial ecosystem that benefits them and their heirs.

All information, content & research in this eBook was derived from ChatGPT AI.

COPYRIGHT 2024

Financial Literacy Group

Ron Harris

info@financialliteracy.group

+1 (323) 419-1600

250 West Ocean Blvd., Ste. 1611

Long Beach, CA 90802

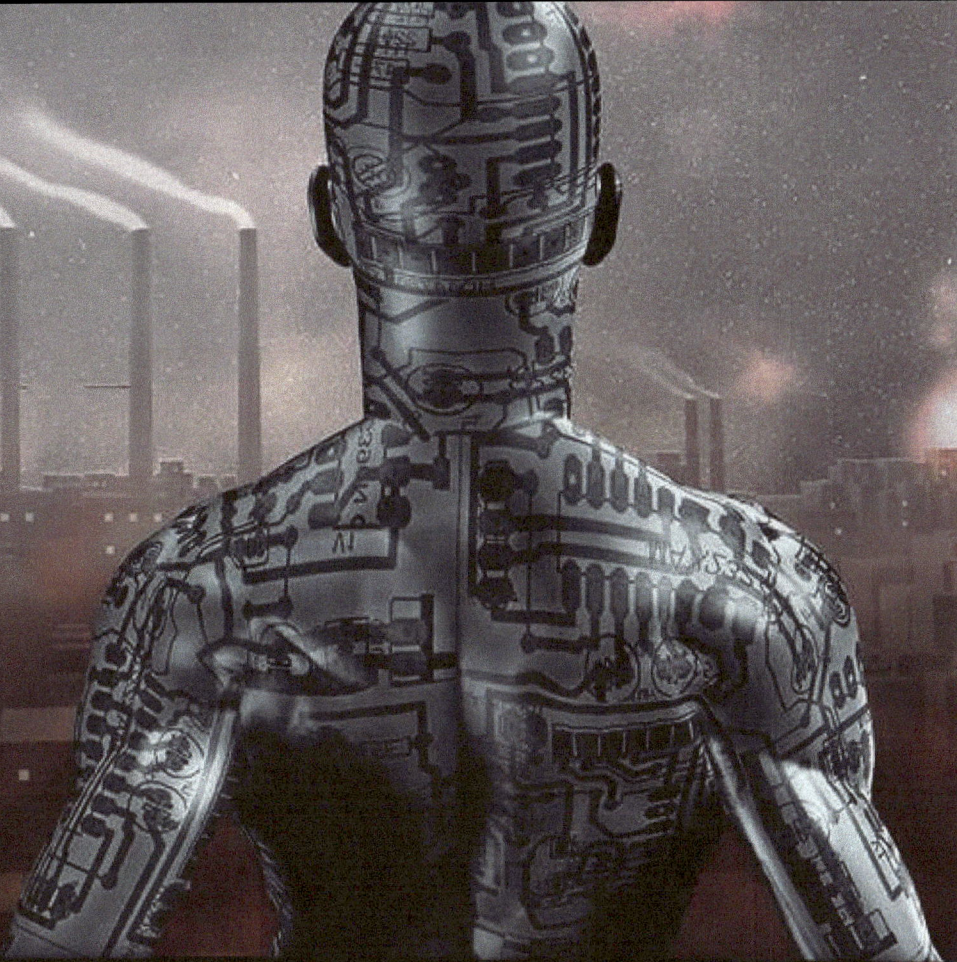

About The Author?

Ron Harris, MBA, MBE, Certified Financial Educator (CFEI), Author, Insurance Professional and CEO of Financial Literacy Group, LLC, was born in Los Angeles, CA. Ron earned a master's degree in global marketing and communications at the University of Essex, UK.

Ron Harris is an entrepreneur who has over 20 years' experience researching, developing integrated sales and marketing strategies that have launched new solutions and technological products for startups, SMEs, and corporations. Ron has worked with companies such as Union Bank of CA, Prudential, KCBS, KCAL, KTLA, FatBurger, the Dial Corporation, Sunkist, MSE, ILG and DocuWise.

For the last 7 years Ron has been helping people on Main Street manage their finances like people who work on Wall St.

Ron has traveled across the US and to over 40 countries to study causes of wealth disparity so that he could apply this knowledge at home in the United States. Ron is dedicated to helping working class people optimize their personal financial positions, improve their lives, retire with dignity and build generational wealth.

All of the information in this e-Book was researched and verified using ChatGPT.

Table Of Contents

The Real World Guide
to Lifetime Retirement Income
for Working Class Americans.

Do you know how much your retirement will cost? Have you considered how you will pay for it? Do you know how to generate the retirement income you will need?

For many current and future retirees, these can be stressful questions that are often put off and left unanswered for too long.

Financial Literacy Group has researched and developed a solution that shows people on main street how to manage they're money like people on wall street. We help our clients with many things, but one of the most important is helping them answer the aforementioned questions and meet their retirement goals.

We've written this guide in an effort to help you answer these fundamental retirement questions for yourself.

Why have we provided this guide at our own expense? We've found educating working class individuals and families is good for our business, whether an individual becomes a client or not. For some, our outstanding client service is an attractive reason to become a client. Others simply want to take our insights and use them on their own. Whichever group you fall into, we sincerely hope this guide helps you reach your retirement goals.

Thank you in advance for the opportuity.

Who We Are?
About Us

What Are Your Retirement Goals?

What is your plan for retirement? Enjoy the golf course? Travel? Spend time with grandchildren? Keep on working, but purely for fun? Building more assets? In our experience, there is immense diversity in how our clients want to spend their retirement. But from a financial perspective, we've found most people are aiming to achieve one (or often more) of the following four goals. And before you focus on anything else, it is imperative you figure out what your goals are for retirement

1. Avoid running out of money?

For many this is their number one goal and their number one retirement fear. Being forced to turn to your children or go back to work during retirement is a source of anxiety for many current and future retirees. Many folks think the key to achieving this goal is low-volatility solutions (e.g., Treasury bonds), but as we will discuss, this is not always the case.

2. Increase wealth?

Some folks are easily able to enjoy the retirement lifestyle of their choosing with no fear of running out of money. For these fortunate individuals, the goal is often to grow their wealth over the long term typically for legacy, whether that's children, grandchildren or charity. Unsurprisingly, most folks with this goal take a growth-oriented approach to their retirement plan.

3. Maintain or improve lifestyle?

Most people have worked hard for their retirement and want to enjoy it. As such, a common goal for many of our clients is to maintain or better yet, improve their lifestyle during retirement. The key there is to maintain or grow purchasing power over time this requires income growth to offset the malicious impact of inflation.

4. Spend every cent?

This isn't a typical goal among our clients, but there are some people who think success is spending all of their money before they die. But this is often can be a risky proposition there's no way to know exactly how long your retirement will last.

The way our solution works we actually want you to spend, because you earn on your spend.

Before you focus on anything else, figure out which of these goals are most important to you. You can't figure out how to get there if you don't know where you are going!

What Will Your Retirement Look Like?

Once you've figured out what your goals are for retirement, you can start to calculate how much your retirement will cost, what will it look like. Four factors to consider are: non-discretionary spending, discretionary spending, inflation and your investment time horizon (e.g., life expectancy).

1. Non-Discretionary Spending

This is the spending you don't have a lot of control over. There may be some wiggle room, but for the most part you can't avoid these costs.

a. Living Expenses: Day-to-day, how much does it cost to maintain your lifestyle? You'll want to consider everything from groceries to gas to the heating bill. If you aren't planning on relocating in retirement, you likely have a good idea of what these expenses look like already.

b. Debt: This can be credit card debt, your mortgage or car loans. Anything you owe needs to be accounted for when mapping out your expenses because you'll have to continue to pay down the principal and make periodic interest payments.

c. Taxes: While taxes are often lower for retirees as they shift from salaried income to capital-gains rates, the government certainly still wants its cut. You may benefit from implementing a strategy to settle your tax bill each year.

d. Insurance and Health Care: Health care costs have historically risen faster than inflation and, for many investors, have become a larger share of their budget in retirement. You'll need to account for insurance payments as well as any emergencies that might require sizable payments on short notice.

2. Non-Discretionary Spending

Once you get past basic living expenses, you have to account for discretionary spending.

Discretionary spending is subject to your personal situation. You may view cable TV as discretionary, but golf as a required, non-discretionary expense.

This is just an example, but the takeaway is if you have a hobby or other expense you can't imagine living without, you'll need to include it in your non-discretionary expenses.

Below are some of the more common discretionary line items in retirees' budgets:

a. Travel: Many people look forward to traveling in retirement. This could include visiting the grandkids or more elaborate trips overseas. If you've been thinking about a dream trip for years, now could be an ideal time to budget for one.

b. Hobbies: Retirement is a great time to rekindle old hobbies or pick up new ones. Ready to finally get your fly casting down or finish researching your family history? Hobbies almost always incur some costs, even if many are small.

c. Luxuries: This is somewhat subject to your own budget and definition of luxury. But whether you enjoy fine wines or simply having coffee out every morning, you'll need to factor non-essential purchases into your expenses.

d. Children and Grandchildren: For many, this last category includes aspects of all the others. Your family could require tuition, travel, luxury purchases and be your favorite hobby all at once. If you need a generous budget to make children and grandchildren a focus in your retirement, you'll need to think about how much cash flow you'll need to support it.

Suitability
Will it Work For You?

Retirement Factors

1. Inflation

Inflation is insidious. It decreases purchasing power over time and erodes real savings and investment returns. Many investors fail to realize how much impact inflation can have. While inflation can fluctuate year to year, since 1925, inflation has averaged about 3% a year.*Even if inflation were to occur at that average rate in the future, a person who currently requires $50,000 to cover annual living expenses would still need approximately $90,000 in 20 years and about $120,000 in 30 years just to maintain the same purchasing power.

2. Retirement Plan Timeline

Your retirement plan time horizon is a major determinant of your total retirement cost and is likely one of the most overlooked factors among today's retirees, fact is, most folks are living longer than they think they will. The retirement plan time horizon can be your life expectancy, the life expectancy of a younger spouse, or a longer or shorter time horizon depending on your investment objectives.

The following table shows total life expectancies for Americans, based on current age. We believe these projections likely underestimate how long people will actually live given ongoing medical advancements.

And don't forget these are projections of average life expectancy, planning for the average is not sufficient because about half of people in each bracket are expected to live even longer. Factors such as current health and heredity can also cause individual life expectancies to vary widely.

The bottom line? Your investment time horizon may be much longer than you realize. Prepare to live a long time and make sure you have enough money to maintain your lifestyle.

Current Age	Life Expectancy	Current Age	Life Expectancy	Current Age	Life Expectancy	Current Age	Life Expectancy
51	82	61	83	71	86	81	90
52	82	62	84	72	86	82	90
53	82	63	84	73	87	83	91
54	82	64	84	74	87	84	91
55	82	65	84	75	87	85	92
56	83	66	85	76	88	86	92
57	83	67	85	77	88	87	93
58	83	68	85	78	88	88	93
59	83	69	85	79	89	89	94
60	83	70	86	80	89	90	95

Your goals, expense needs and time horizon all factor into how you should approach generating income in retirement. Next, let's examine some techniques you can consider for getting the cash flow you need.

*Source: FactSet, as of 3/15/2023. US BLS Consumer Price Index from 12/31/1925 – 12/31/2022.

**Source: Social Security as of 3/15/2023. Period Life Table, 2019, as used in the 2022 Trustees Report. Life expectancy rounded to nearest year

How Will You Pay for Retirement?

Once you have a sense of how much your retirement will cost, you can start figuring out how you're going to pay for it. We suggest you calculate all of the income you generate without relying on your investments. The most common categories of non-investment income are listed below

1. Non-Investment Income

Salary: Will you work at all in retirement? If so, you'll need to estimate how much salary you can expect. For our purposes, don't count money you make from a business investment or partnership; just consider direct financial transfers from your employer to you.

Social Security: If you've started taking Social Security, you're likely familiar with how much to expect. If you haven't yet, you may want to determine the age you want to start receiving benefits and how much you should expect monthly. The Social Security Administration's website has a free calculator* you can use to estimate your future payments.

Pension: If your employer offers a pension, you should determine how much you can expect to receive on a regular basis. Will it increase or decrease over time? Note, 401(k)s and IRAs are not pension plans. Rather, they are types of accounts that hold funds you've invested over the years and will be able to control in retirement.

Business and Real Estate: If you maintain an interest in a business or investment property, this could produce non-investment income. When calculating how much to expect, consider these sources of income are often more susceptible to market conditions than Social Security or a guaranteed pension.

Are You Financially Well?
Financial Well Being

Not Saving Enough For Retirement?

As of our last statistical update in 2023, the question of whether Americans are saving enough for retirement is complex and varies widely based on individual circumstances. However, several general trends and factors can be considered:

1. Retirement Savings Statistics: Many Americans are not saving enough for retirement. Surveys have often shown that a significant portion of the population has little to no retirement savings. Factors like income level, financial literacy, and access to retirement savings plans play a significant role.

2. Impact of Debt on Retirement Savings: High levels of debt, especially high-interest debt like credit card debt, can severely impact an individual's ability to save for retirement. Debt payments can take a large portion of income that could otherwise be directed towards retirement savings. Additionally, the stress of managing debt can lead people to delay or minimize their retirement contributions.

Retirement Vehicles Are Not Enough!

1. Retirement Savings Vehicles:
    a. 401(k)s: These are popular retirement savings vehicles, especially for employees of private-sector companies. They offer tax advantages and often employer matching, but are limited by contribution limits and sometimes by the investment options available.

    b. IRAs (Individual Retirement Accounts): These accounts offer tax advantages and are available to most earners and their spouses. They are more flexible in terms of investment choices but have lower annual contribution limits compared to 401(k)s.

    c. TSPs (Thrift Savings Plans): Similar to 401(k)s, but for federal employees and members of the uniformed services, TSPs offer low-cost investment options and matching contributions.

1. Turning Debt and Liabilities into Income and Wealth: The concept of transforming debt into income or wealth often involves strategies like debt consolidation, refinancing, or investing in assets that generate income (such as rental properties). While these strategies can be effective, they often require a level of financial literacy and stability not available to all individuals. For example, investing in real estate to generate rental income can be a way to build wealth, but it also requires capital and risk tolerance.

2. Alternative Perspectives and New Strategies: Some financial experts advocate for more innovative and aggressive investment strategies, or for broader systemic changes to improve retirement security. For example, there's ongoing debate about whether the traditional advice of prioritizing low-risk investments as one ages is always the best route, especially in an era of longer life expectancies and potentially lower returns on conservative investments.

3. Policy and Education: Improving access to retirement savings plans, especially for workers in small businesses or gig economy jobs, along with better financial education, are often cited as key steps towards improving the retirement readiness of Americans.

4. Personalized Financial Planning: Ultimately, each individual's situation is unique, and retirement planning should ideally be tailored to personal circumstances, including income, debt levels, family obligations, health considerations, and retirement goals.

In conclusion, while 401(k)s, IRAs, and TSPs are adequate vehicles for saving money for retirement, their effectiveness can be influenced by factors like personal debt, investment choices, and overall financial planning. The idea of turning debt into wealth is intriguing but requires careful management and a certain level of financial acumen.

Download Now!
Bank Like a Bank App

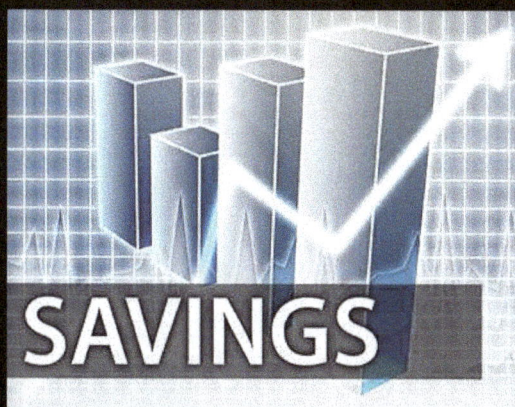

SAVINGS

Stock Market Has Not Been Favorable?

The relationship between the stock market and the middle class, particularly in the context of the United States, is multifaceted and complex. Here's an analysis covering various aspects of the question:

1. Stock Market and the Middle Class

a. 401(k)s, IRAs, and Retirement Accounts: These investment vehicles are heavily tied to the stock market. They have become a primary means of retirement savings for the middle class, especially after the decline of defined-benefit pension plans. When the stock market performs well, these accounts generally grow, potentially benefiting middle-class retirement security. However, market downturns can significantly impact these savings.

b. Investment Education and Access: There's often a knowledge gap in understanding stock market investments, which can affect how effectively individuals use these tools for retirement savings. While higher-income individuals may have more access to financial advice and resources, the middle class might not always have the same level of guidance, potentially affecting their investment outcomes.

c. Volatility and Risk: The stock market is inherently volatile. This volatility can be a double-edged sword for middle-class investors who might not have the resources to withstand significant downturns, especially if they are close to retirement age.

2. Effect of Wall Street on Middle-Class Retirement

a. Growth and Risk: While the stock market can provide opportunities for wealth growth, it also exposes retirement savings to market risk. The 2008 financial crisis, for instance, saw significant declines in the value of retirement accounts, highlighting this vulnerability.

b. Dependence on Market Performance: As retirement savings are increasingly linked to market performance, middle-class retirees may face uncertainty, depending on market conditions at the time of their retirement.

Let's Talk?
Set An Appoinment

Retirement Now Is More Difficult?

1. Are Retirement Accounts Good for the Middle Class?

a. Long-term Growth Potential: Historically, investing in the stock market has yielded higher long-term returns compared to traditional savings methods. This aspect can be beneficial for retirement savings.

b. Tax Advantages: Many retirement accounts offer tax benefits, either on the contributions (traditional IRAs and 401(k)s) or on withdrawals (Roth IRAs), which can be advantageous for middle-class savers.

c. Diversification and Access: These accounts often allow for diversification of investments, which is crucial for managing risk. They also democratize access to the stock market for the middle class.

2. Is the Middle Class Growing?

a. Economic and Social Shifts: The size and economic health of the middle class are influenced by broader economic trends, including wage growth, job market changes, cost of living, and educational opportunities. Over the past few decades, there have been concerns about the shrinking middle class in the U.S., often attributed to factors like income inequality and stagnating wages.

b. Recent Trends: As of the last update in 2023, there were indications of both growth and challenges for the middle class. The specific trajectory is influenced by current economic policies, globalization, technological changes, and other socio-economic factors.

3. Current State of America's Middle Class

a. Economic Pressures: The middle class has faced various challenges such as rising healthcare costs, higher education expenses, and housing affordability. These factors can strain middle-class finances, impacting their ability to save for retirement.

b. Income Stagnation vs. Cost of Living: In many cases, middle-class incomes have not kept pace with the rising cost of living, affecting their economic stability and ability to accumulate wealth.

c. Wealth Inequality: There is a growing disparity in wealth distribution, with a significant portion of stock market gains accruing to the wealthiest individuals. This disparity can impact the relative benefit the middle class receives from stock market growth.

d. Policy and Support: Government policies, including tax laws and retirement savings incentives, play a significant role in shaping the economic well-being of the middle class. The effectiveness of these policies in supporting middle-class retirement security is a subject of ongoing debate.

The difference between your total income and your total expenses is your net savings. If this is negative (as it is for many retirees), you'll need more cash flow from your life insurance to ensure you're able to cover all of your expenses. This guide primarily focuses on generating cash flow from your life insurance and annuities to bridge this gap. But before we get into specific strategies, we discuss some important principles of retirement investing.

Conclusion

In summary, while the stock market and investment vehicles like 401(k)s and IRAs offer opportunities for wealth accumulation and retirement savings for the middle class, they also come with risks and challenges. The overall impact on the middle class depends on a range of factors, including market performance, economic policies, individual financial literacy and investment strategies. The state of America's middle class is dynamic, influenced by broader economic trends and policies.

Download Now!
Bank Like a Bank App

We Pay For Advice & Market Insights?

Whether middle-class individuals can become rich by investing in the stock market is a nuanced question and depends on various factors. Here are some key points to consider:

1. Long-Term Investing: Historically, the stock market has provided returns that outpace inflation over the long term. Middle-class investors who consistently invest in a diversified portfolio for many years may see significant growth in their investments.
2. Compound Interest: One of the most powerful tools in investing is compound interest. The earlier and more consistently one invests, the more time their investments have to grow.
3. Investment Strategy: Success in the stock market often depends on the investor's strategy. Index funds or mutual funds, which represent a diversified portfolio, tend to be less risky compared to individual stocks but might offer more moderate returns.
4. Risk Tolerance: Individual stocks can provide high returns, but they come with higher risk. Understanding and being comfortable with one's risk tolerance is crucial.
5. Market Volatility: The stock market can be unpredictable in the short term. Investors who are successful in growing wealth typically do not panic in downturns and maintain their investment strategy.
6. Savings Rate: The amount of money one can invest plays a significant role. A higher savings rate can potentially lead to greater wealth accumulation.
7. Financial Education: Understanding the stock market, investment options, tax implications, and investment fees can significantly impact investment outcomes.
8. Income Level: While it's possible for middle-class individuals to accumulate wealth over time through the stock market, the initial amount of disposable income available for investment can be a limiting factor.
9. Time Horizon: The amount of time one has to invest impacts the potential for wealth growth. Younger investors typically have a longer time horizon, allowing for more aggressive investment strategies.
10. Lifestyle and Spending: Personal financial management, such as maintaining a reasonable lifestyle and avoiding high debt, also plays a crucial role in wealth accumulation.

It's important to remember that investing in the stock market involves risk, and it's possible to lose money. Therefore, it's advisable to consult with a financial advisor or conduct thorough personal research before making investment decisions. Additionally, becoming "rich" is a relative term and varies based on individual financial goals and definitions of wealth.

Get Insights?
No Charge

How Investment Advisors Make Money?

Investment advisors, brokers, and financial planners have different ways of making money, and their income may or may not be directly tied to the performance of their clients' investments. Here's a breakdown:

1. Commission-Based Model: Brokers typically work on a commission basis. They earn money by selling financial products like stocks, bonds, mutual funds, and insurance. Whether or not the client makes money, the broker earns a commission on the transactions. This can sometimes lead to a conflict of interest if the broker is incentivized to sell products that are not in the client's best interest.

2. Fee-Based Model: Many investment advisors and some financial planners use a fee-based model. This can include a combination of fees for advice and commissions on product sales. The fee might be a flat rate, an hourly rate, or a percentage of the assets under management (AUM). If the fee is AUM-based, the advisor earns more as the client's assets grow, which can align the advisor's interests with the client's success. However, they may still earn this fee even in periods when the client's investments do not perform well.

3. Fee-Only Model: Fee-only financial planners and advisors charge only for their advice and do not earn commissions on product sales. Their income is typically derived from flat fees, hourly rates, or a percentage of the assets they manage. Like the fee-based model, if they charge a percentage of AUM, their income can fluctuate with the value of their client's portfolio, aligning their interests with the client's investment performance. However, they also earn their fees regardless of the portfolio's performance.

4. Performance-Based Fees: Some investment advisors, particularly those managing hedge funds or certain types of private investment funds, might charge performance-based fees. This means they earn a fee only if the investments exceed a certain benchmark or hurdle rate. This model closely aligns the advisor's earnings with the client's investment performance.

5. Other Revenue Streams: Some advisors and planners might also earn money from other services such as financial planning, consulting, or offering educational workshops.

It's important for clients to understand how their financial professionals are compensated, as this can influence the recommendations and advice they provide. Transparency in fees and compensation is crucial in ensuring that the advice given is in the best interest of the client.

Advisors Charge Fees!

Investment fees are fees charged to use financial products, such as broker fees, trading fees, and expense ratios. Investment and advisor fees are charges that investors pay for professional advice and management of their financial assets.

Investment fees are one of the most important determinants of investment performance and are something on which every investor should focus. Understanding these fees is crucial for investors, as they can significantly impact the overall returns on investments.

Over time, minimizing fees tends to maximize performance. However, it is important not to let fees dominate your investment decision-making process. Here's a detailed overview:

1. Investment Fees: These are fees associated with the purchase, holding, and sale of investment products like mutual funds, ETFs, stocks, bonds, and other securities. These fees are usually a percentage of the investment amount or a fixed transaction fee.

2. Advisor Fees: These are charges for professional financial advice and portfolio management services. Advisors may charge fees for developing financial plans, offering investment recommendations, and managing assets.

3. Broker Fees: These are fees charged by a broker for executing transactions or providing specialized services. For example, when you buy or sell a stock, your broker might charge a transaction fee.

4. Trading Fees: Similar to broker fees, these are cost

5. Expense Ratios: This is a common fee associated with mutual funds and ETFs (exchange-traded funds). The expense ratio is an annual fee expressed as a percentage of the fund's total assets and covers the fund's operational expenses, including management, administration, marketing, and distribution.

6. Management Fees: For managed portfolios or investment advice, you might pay a management fee, usually a percentage of the assets under management. This fee compensates the investment manager for their expertise and time.

7. Load Fees: These are charged by some mutual funds and are a type of sales charge. A front-end load is charged when you buy shares, and a back-end load is charged when you sell shares.

8. Performance Fees: Some funds charge a fee based on the fund's performance relative to a benchmark.

9. Other Costs: These might include custodian fees, legal and auditing fees, and other administrative expenses.

Watch Video
About Fees

How Do Fees Work?

1. Investment Fees: If you invest in a mutual fund with an annual expense ratio of 1%, and you have $10,000 invested in the fund, you will pay $100 in fees per year.
2. Advisor Fees: If a financial advisor charges a 1% annual fee and manages a portfolio of $100,000 for you, you will pay $1,000 in advisory fees per year.

1. Types

a. Transaction Fees: Charged per trade or transaction (buying/selling securities).

b. Expense Ratios: Annual fees as a percentage of assets invested in mutual funds or ETFs.

c. Management Fees: Ongoing fees charged by financial advisors or robo-advisors, usually a percentage of the assets under management.

d. Front-End Loads: Fees paid when purchasing shares of a mutual fund.

e. Back-End Loads: Fees incurred when selling shares of a mutual fund.

f. Performance Fees: Additional fees charged by some funds or advisors based on the fund's or portfolio's performance.

g. Commission Fees: Charged by brokers for buying or selling securities.

2. Cost

a. Average Cost:
Mutual fund expense ratios can range from below 0.10% to over 2% annually.
Financial advisors typically charge between 0.25% and 1% of assets under management annually.
Commissions for stock trades can vary widely, though many platforms now offer commission-free trading.
b. Impact on Returns: High fees can significantly erode investment returns over time. For example, a 1% annual fee can reduce the final amount of a long-term investment by a significant percentage over several decades.
Fees reduce your overall return. For example, if your investment gains 8% in a year but you pay 1% in fees, your net return is 7%.
The long-term impact of fees can be substantial due to the compound effect. Even a small difference in fees can lead to a significant difference in returns over an extended period.

Considerations:

Fee Structures: Understand the difference between fee-only and commission-based advisors.
Total Expense Ratio (TER): Look at the total cost of owning an investment, including all fees.
Value for Money: Assess whether the advice and services provided justify the fees.
Fee Transparency: Ensure that all fees are disclosed and understood before investing.

While investment and advisor fees are an essential part of the financial services industry, investors must be aware of the types and costs of these fees to make informed decisions and to ensure that their investments grow efficiently over time.

In summary, while focusing on minimizing investment fees is wise, investors should also consider other factors such as investment goals, risk tolerance, and the quality of the investment or service they are receiving.

Learn More
About Fees

How Investment Companies Get Paid?

Investing in various financial instruments and entities like mutual funds, ETFs, stocks, bonds, and investment companies involves different strategies and sources of income. Here's a basic overview of how each typically makes money:

1. Mutual Funds:

a. Income from Dividends and Interest: Mutual funds earn money from dividends on stocks and interest on bonds held in their portfolios. Investors in the fund typically receive these earnings as fund distributions.

b. Capital Gains: When a mutual fund sells securities that have increased in price, the fund has a capital gain. These gains are often distributed to investors.

c. Increase in NAV (Net Asset Value): If the market value of a fund's portfolio increases after accounting for expenses and liabilities, the NAV per share increases, which benefits investors if they sell their shares at a higher NAV than the purchase price.

2. Exchange-Traded Funds (ETFs):

a. Dividend Income and Interest: Similar to mutual funds, ETFs earn income from dividends on stocks and interest from bonds in their portfolios.

b. Capital Gains: ETFs also make money through capital gains when the underlying assets in the fund increase in value. However, ETFs are often more tax-efficient with capital gains due to their unique creation and redemption mechanism.

c. Trading at Market Value: Unlike mutual funds, ETFs are traded on stock exchanges and can be bought and sold at market price, which can fluctuate throughout the trading day.

3. Stocks:

a. Dividends: Some stocks provide income through dividends, which are a portion of a company's earnings distributed to shareholders.

b. Capital Appreciation: Investors can make money from stocks if the stock's price increases over time and they sell it for more than they paid.

3. Bonds:

a. Interest Payments: Bonds typically pay regular interest to the bondholder. This interest is known as the coupon.

b. Capital Gains: If a bond is sold before its maturity date for a price higher than the purchase price, the investor can realize a capital gain.

4. Investment Companies/Corporations

a. Asset Appreciation: If the assets owned by the investment company (like stocks, bonds, real estate, etc.) increase in value, the value of the company and consequently its stock may increase.

b. Dividends and Interest: These companies may also earn income from dividends and interest from their investm1ents, which can be passed on to shareholders.

c. Fees and Commissions: Some investment companies make money through fees and commissions for services provided to clients.

Each type of investment has its own risk profile and potential for returns, and they can serve different roles in an investment portfolio depending on an investor's goals, risk tolerance, and investment horizon.

Watch Video?
How it Works

So, Have We Been Fooled?

How did it get like this? Part of this reason is that we have been trained by our society & the financial institutions, to think the way they want us to. They hide the chinks in their armor, we don't ask the important questions and we don't see what they don't want us to see. Most of us don't:

> Question: paying a fully amortized mortgage for 30 years.
> Have any idea how to cancel interest?
> Know how credit card companies change the interest rate.
> Have any idea how minimum payments are calculated?
> Realize that insurance policies can be used to pay debt.
> Comprehend the full benefits of a life Insurance policy.
> Understand what it means to be your own bank.
> Realize that what the banks do to us is reciprocal.
> Know the difference between recourse and nonrecourse loans?
> Don't read the small print on credit contracts or documents.

If we play the game on the financial institution's field and by their rules, then we are playing their game. They are not the only game in town.

But when we start to think outside of that box financially, our friends and relatives tell us it is not possible, so we start to doubt it, even if we know it is possible. Then, you see a billboard, a commercial or your bank sends you an email with a discount, that is actually meaningless, but consumers inherently trust them because that is the way things are done. Wealthy people aren't marketed to, the way the masses are. Financial institutions market to the masses, with paths that make people "feel" wealthy and successful, just let the bank handle your finances and you'll be fine.

Our friends, however, are not experts, in most cases. financial institutions, large corporations, media & the rich, manipulate us into not looking in the right places, for solutions to our problems. So, if you feel the effects of high-cost, low-quality financial instruments and lack of transparency about your finances, you are not alone.

Think about it! How many American families are really prepared to spend 5 years of retirement living on $1,000 per month? Is refinancing a student loan with So-Fi a solution? Our society & financial institutions teach us to have a certain way of thinking about money.

So we live paycheck to paycheck, like it is normal. We're in debt and we accept it. We have trouble with credit cards, but we keep spending. We don't know how to manage our finances, and we think there is no real way to change things. Unless you inherit wealth, a solid plan for building generational wealth with persistent cash flow is instrumental.

Look, we know that people buy things they don't need, with money they don't have, to impress people they don't know, and we're not trying to blame the situation solely on the banks.

In either case, traditional financial institutions are working hard, to pull consumers further and further into debt, creating a vicious cycle for the economy and for millions of American families.

Free Your Mind

And Your Cash Will Follow?

The problems we have with banking, the credit card industry, mortgages, and student debt are all because most of us don't know how these mechanisms work.

We don't really understand how life insurance works, while the people who do prosper. We would know if we had been taught these things in high school. Unfortunately, their main purpose was to make money for the financial institutions that set up these solutions and sold them. Money is constantly occupying our minds.

From policy makers, to businesses, to the media, there are constant forces influencing us.

Americans are hurting financially, and need to change their mindset, they need to break out of this cycle, take control of their money and start achieving a common goal of saving money..

We live in one of the most advanced societies in the world, and with all the technological, social, and medical advances we have made, we still cannot manage our money effectively.

So many people have no idea how to make the most of their money, and with all the noise out there, we are paralyzed, in fact, we wouldn't recognize or trust a good solution if it fell in our laps.

If enough people stop using credit cards, if more people pay off their mortgages quicker, our economy could ease itself from its slow rot of infinite debt and perpetual economic crisis. However, the banks, media, and the government all tell us we must have a 401K in our retirement plans, but a 401K will most likely run out of money, earlier than we think.

Here's a question; Do you think interest rates will go up or down in the future? If we can't take care of our personal finances today, how will we deal with inflation tomorrow?

It's time to find out how we can use all the tools and resources available. Our elected officials require financial institutions to explain and teach us real information. Not just take our money. We have a right to understand how our finances work.

But don't hold your breath hoping that will happen, in the meantime you know how it goes. Life gets stressful. Bills pile up on the table. You feel like you're barely making ends meet each month. But this time you can learn a new way out! There are real solutions out there. You can really get out of debt.

Your mortgage can be paid in as little as 5 years. You can still retire with dignity. So, are you going to take the red or the blue pill?

Many of the techniques here in this eBook have been used for years by rich professionals, they understand how money works. The other solutions in this eBook have been created by us, they take advantage of all the hacks and the loopholes available.

This book was written to start a conversation, a transformation of thought by educating the everyday American, about how an empowered society functions with a stimulus of knowledge. As the old saying goes, it takes a village, but in this situation, the village working to close the gap is connected locally and digitally. Communities must work together at achieving this common goal

Set Appointment
Book US

We Already Understood The Problem!

We start with financial education; our eLearning courses play a large role in staging the overall direction of each customized program. It starts with a pre-test to develop a snapshot of a student's basic personal finance knowledge. This is followed by a comprehensive course and then a final exam to determine how effective the course was.

Our how money Works eLearning course equips the user with the knowledge and skills to be able to make sound financial decisions that will help them manage money more effectively. It not only shows the user how money works, but it shows the user how money is made, spent, saved, and grown. Courses are produced in English and Spanish.

Consumers that take our online courses generally become better at making financial decisions and they learn that their money can work for them.

eLearning courses deliver real-world financial management concepts that increase the literacy of middle-class adults. The quizzes provide a pathway for students to see progress and the online format means that students work at their own pace. The website allows courses to be translated into multiple languages, via Google translate.

This interactive multimedia course, designed to help students come to grips with their personal financial position, teaches the student how to manage their money, budget, savings, interest, debt and how life insurance or proper protection works, and why it is so important.

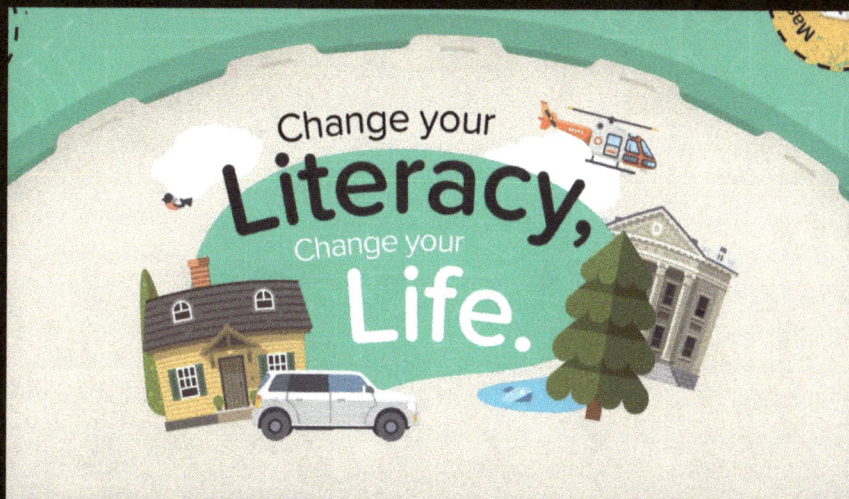

Change your Literacy, Change your Life.

a. Think Like the Wealthy

b. Sucker Cycle

c. Compound Interest

d. Time Value of Money

e. Million Dollar Baby

f. The Rule of 72

g. 7 Money Milestones

h. Financial Education

i. Proper Protection

j. Emergency Fund

k. Debt Management

l. Increase Cash Flow

m. Build Wealth

n. Protect Wealth

View Our Courses?
eLearning

High Interest Prohibits Wealth Building!

Using the GPS Debt Mapping Technology generally causes users to become better at making financial decisions and they learn that their money can work for them.

This sophisticated technology serves as a financial GPS that directs the user to pay off a 30-year mortgage in as little as 5-7 years, with no change to your budget.

People who use this smart debt elimination tool will save up to 70% of the interest on their 1st and/or 2nd mortgage, without changing their budget. GPS Debt Mapping Technology shows the user the exact date they will be debt free and its debt reduction results are guaranteed.

The technology works on both secured and unsecured debt; credit cards, residential and commercial mortgages, auto, equity, personal, student, equipment, and business loans. The technology can manage multiple mortgages and all personal and/or business debt simultaneously, it can also be securely connected to most bank accounts.

The technology prioritizes your debt and pays the most costly loans first and continues this method until all the user's debt is completely paid off. GPS Debt Mapping Technology uses an algorithm-based method that maximizes 4 key money-saving principles; strategic payoff, interest accumulation, interest float, and interest cancellation. The solution is programmed to guide the user to eliminate debt in record time.

This is a game-changing technology. Being able to pay a mortgage in as little as 5-7 years means that a baby boomer in his 60s still has time to buy a home. This solution gets the user to equity faster, to more savings, more disposable income, better credit ratings, more money for investing and more money for retirement, simply more wealth.

GPS Debt Mapping Technology uses an intelligent digital interactive mobile financial planner, educator, and guide that keeps the user on track, prompting them to follow the optimized road map to debt freedom. This includes payments, account or money movement, step-by-step instructions, as well as the dates and times those payments or moves need to be made.

A user can enter a potential purchase into the solution to see its true consequences, interest and debt implications, as well as the effect the purchase will have on their net worth. The solution also shows the user how they can quickly pay off new loans or a future purchase, and it adjusts to the new date in which the user will now become debt free. Below is an example of the results in an average debt case, when the GPS Debt Technology is used.

Learn More
Debt Mapping

For:	**Prepared By: Financial Literacy Group**	**Page 1**
	ron@financialliteracy.group / (323) 419-1600	Wed Aug 26, 2020

Summary of Debts

Name	Balance	Rate	Payment
Mortgage Debt (1)	$987,280.46	3.50 %	$4,490.45
Loans (2)	$97,642.24	2.68 %	$1,540.06
Credit Cards (3)	$3.00	18.16 %	$3.00
Total	**$1,084,925.70**	**3.43 %**	**$6,033.51**

Discretionary Income Analysis

Description	Amount	% of Income
Base Monthly Income	$15,000.00	100.0 %
Monthly Debt Payments	$6,033.56	40.2 %
Other Monthly Expenses	$5,379.49	35.9 %
Monthly Discretionary Income	**$3,586.95**	**23.9 %**

Having debt is no walk in the park!

This month you'll pay *over $3,000 in interest alone*. That's *51 %* of your monthly payment *...gone!*

On average over the next *29.3 years* your bank's plan will cost you *more than $1,700 per month* in interest.

You'll spend *$2.79* for every *$1* you pay down in principal on your mortgage this month.

It will be *June 2037* (16.9 years from now) before you have paid off *half* of your debt and you will still owe *over $542,000*.

What The Money Max Account can do for you

Your Bank's Plan	vs	The Money Max Account	=	You Save

Total Debt Payments

$1,686,015	vs	$1,261,767	=	$424,248
That's 55 % more than your current outstanding balance of $1,084,926!		*This is the total amount you will pay to completely eliminate all of your listed debts.*		*That's a BIG TIP for the bank! Let's make it 112 payments of $3,788.*

Total Interest Payments

$601,090	vs	$176,841	=	$424,248
That's 3.3 years worth of your entire income of $15,000/month just to cover the interest!		*You would need an interest rate of 1.03 % to pay this little interest on a new 30-year loan!*		*Save 71 % in interest or 2.4 years worth of your entire income!*

Projected Payoff

29.3 years	vs	9.3 years	=	19.9 years
With 351 payments to go you'll still be making payments in the year 2049!		*You'll be debt-free by November 2029 after only 112 payments.*		*What could you do with 239 months with NO monthly debt payments?*

Wealth Accumulation

$0	vs	$2,873,521	=	$2,873,521
You'll be making debt payments for the next 29 years instead of building wealth.		*With Money Max Account, we'll use your 19.9 years saved to start building wealth!*		*This is your savings with a 1 % return. Imagine your savings at higher rates!*

Why wait? Start saving today!

By getting started today you can save *over $424,000* in interest payments over the next 9.3 years.

By saving *19.9 years* of debt payments you could build *more than $2,873,000* in wealth over that same time period!

Each month you delay getting started will cost you *$3,788* on average over the next 9.3 years! *Don't wait! Start now!*

Debt-Free In	Debt-Free By	Years Saved	Total Savings	Avg. Savings/Mo
9.3 years	**Nov-2029**	**19.9**	**$424,248**	**$3,788**

Mortgage Pay Off No HELOC Needed!

This debt payoff strategy that is effective without the need for a home equity line of credit (HELOC), changes in budget, or lifestyle alterations.

No Use of HELOC: Avoiding a Home Equity Line of Credit (HELOC) suggests that this strategy isn't about consolidating debt or using home equity to pay off other debts. This is generally a prudent approach, as it avoids putting your home at risk.

The Dodd-Frank Act and the role of the Consumer Financial Protection Bureau (CFPB), it is correct that these regulations have significantly impacted the mortgage industry. The Dodd-Frank Act aimed to reduce risks in the financial system following the 2008 financial crisis. Part of its mandate was to address issues in the mortgage market, which was a key factor in the crisis.

The CFPB rules that took effect in 2014 include several important provisions:

1. Ability-to-Repay and Qualified Mortgage Standards: Lenders must make a reasonable and good faith determination that the borrower has the ability to repay the loan. This includes considering factors like income, assets, employment, and debt-to-income ratio.

2. Prohibiting Excessive Prepayment Penalties: As mentioned, the CFPB rules restrict prepayment penalties on most residential mortgages. This means that borrowers can pay off their mortgages early without facing steep penalties, which could be beneficial in a debt payoff strategy.

3. Rules for Servicers: The CFPB also established new rules for mortgage servicers, focusing on clear communication with borrowers and proper handling of payments, error resolution, and dealing with struggling borrowers.

Remember, while innovative debt repayment strategies can be helpful, they should always be approached with caution and a good understanding of the details and potential risks involved.

Watch Video
Testimonials

The Catalyst For What Came Next?

1. CARES Act 2020

a. The CARES Act, passed in 2020, brought several changes to the IRS codes 7702 and 101(a), which impacted the Index Universal Life (IUL) insurance policies, along with other life insurance policies.

b. Changes to retirement accounts and insurance policies to provide financial relief during the COVID-19 pandemic. However, the effect was indirect, it didn't directly alter the IRS codes 7702 and 101(a).

c. IRS Code 7702 defines what constitutes a life insurance contract for tax purposes. It sets the minimum death benefit that a policy must have relative to its cash value to qualify as a life insurance contract and receive tax advantages, like tax-free death benefits and deferred cash value growth.

d. IRS Code 101(a) generally states that death benefits paid by a life insurance policy are not included in the gross income of the recipient, and therefore not subject to income tax.

e. Index Universal Life (IUL) Insurance is a type of permanent life insurance policy that has a cash value component, which can be invested in index-linked options. IUL policies provide a death benefit and also have a cash value component that grows on a tax deferred basis.

f. The cash value in an IUL policy can be accessed via policy loans or withdrawals. Policy loans are generally not taxable, as they are considered debts, not distributions. However, if the policy lapses or is surrendered with a loan outstanding, the loan balance becomes taxable.

2. The Effect of The Cares Act

a. Index Universal Life Insurance: This is a type of permanent life insurance that also offers a cash value component that can grow over time. The cash value can be invested in index options (e.g., S&P 500) and grows tax-deferred. You can take loans against the cash value, which are not taxable. The changes to the IRS codes 7702 and 101(a) impacted the minimum interest rates used for calculating the premiums and cash values of these policies, which could potentially allow for higher cash value accumulation.

b. The Cares Act Allows an IUL to Duplicate a Bank: In the Cares Act scenario the IUL created for Hybrid Arbitrage is similar to a Bank Owned Life Insurance (BOLI), the owner can borrow against the money used to overfund the IUL policy (i.e., the cash value), they are not borrowing against the death benefit. This BOLI style IUL is liquid, without surrender charges, or caps, the owner's liabilities can be used to overfund the policy.

3. Why is This Not More Widely Known

The differences between these options are not widely known or understood by most consumers because financial products can be complex and challenging to understand without a thorough explanation from a knowledgeable source. Additionally, most life insurance or financial advisors may not educate clients on these options because they may not be well-versed in the intricacies of life insurance products, or they may have a bias towards products that they commonly sell or that provide them with higher commissions.

It is crucial to work with a financial professional who understands your financial situation, goals, and is knowledgeable about a wide range of financial products to get the most appropriate advice for your situation.

This is why we suggest that you work with FLGPE (Financial Literacy Group Professional Educator), they are trained on the specifics of Banking Like a Bank and using IULs

Learn More
Cares Act 2020

The Comparison Was Overwelming?

1. Risk: The IUL has the least risk among the three due to the guaranteed minimum interest rate (floor). 401(k) and IRAs carry market risk, which means they can lose value if the market performs poorly.

2. Taxation: 401(k) and Traditional IRA allow for tax-deductible contributions, while IUL and Roth IRA do not. However, IUL and Roth IRA allow for tax-free withdrawals up to a certain amount, while 401(k) and Traditional IRA do not.

3. Utilization: Money in a 401K or an IRA cannot be accessed early without penalties. With liquid IUL the cash value can be accessed and used to pay debt early, canceling interest.

4. Investment Options: IRAs offer the most investment options, followed by 401(k)s. IULs have limited investment options, usually linked to a stock market index.

5. Wealth Accumulation: While the IUL offers a guaranteed minimum interest rate, it also usually has a cap on the maximum return, but in the case of Hybrid Arbitrage there are no caps on the IUL, which means there is no limit to wealth accumulation in years when the stock market performs exceptionally well. 401(k)s and IRAs do not have a cap on returns, but also do not have a guaranteed minimum interest rate.

Watch 3 Minute Video?
401K, IRA, IUL Comparison

The Benefits Were Overwelming!

1. Purpose:

IUL: Provides a death benefit, the funds from an IUL policy can be used for any purpose including debt elimination and the opportunity for cash value accumulation. The benefits of using debt to reduce the pay-off time and interest, also known as "debt elimination," involve using the cash value of an IUL policy to pay down debt while continuing to earn interest on the borrowed amount. This strategy aims to optimize cash flow, minimize interest paid, and increase wealth accumulation because the tax-free loans never have to be paid back.

401(k) and IRA: Primarily designed for retirement savings, whereas there might be penalties for early withdrawals or non-qualified expenses from a 401K or IRA

2. Investment Limit:

IUL: There is no legal limit on the amount you can invest in an IUL policy. No legal limit on the premium, but it must be within the boundaries set by IRS Code 7702.

401(k) and IRA: There are annual contribution limits for 401K and IRA accounts.

3. Tax Advantages:

IUL: The cash value grows deferred, and loans are generally not taxable. The tax status doesn't change unless the policy lapses or is surrendered with an outstanding loan.

401(k) and IRA: Contributions are tax-deductible, and investments grow tax-deferred, but withdrawals in retirement are subject to income tax.

4. Longevity:

IUL: Is a permanent life insurance policy, it lasts your entire lifetime, as long as premiums are paid.

401(k) and IRA: Accounts do not offer any life insurance component and can be depleted if withdrawals exceed the growth of the investments.

Watch 9 Minute Video?
401K, IRA, IUL Comparison

Turn Debt Into Income & Wealth!

Overfunding a life insurance policy up to the Modified Endowment Contract (MEC) limit and then borrowing against its cash value to pay off debts like mortgages and loans is a strategy some individuals use for financial planning. Here's an overview of how this works and its implications:

1. Life Insurance Policy with Cash Value: This strategy typically involves a whole life insurance policy or a universal life insurance policy, which not only provides a death benefit but also accumulates cash value over time. The cash value grows tax-deferred.

2. Overfunding Up to MEC Limit: You can pay premiums into the policy beyond the amount needed to keep it in force. However, if these payments exceed certain limits, the policy can become a Modified Endowment Contract (MEC), changing its tax treatment. Staying below the MEC limit is crucial to maintain favorable tax treatment.

3. Borrowing Against Cash Value: Instead of borrowing against the face value (the death benefit), you're borrowing against the cash value that the policy has accumulated (Liabilities or debt). This is essentially a loan from the insurance company, using your policy's cash value as collateral.

4. Interest on the Loan: The insurance company will charge interest on the loan. The rate is set by the policy terms. You are, in essence, paying interest to the insurance company. However the cash value of the policy is indexing and continuing to earn interest.

5. Repayment of the Loan: The loan doesn't necessarily have to be repaid. However, if it's not repaid, the unpaid amount (plus interest) will be deducted from the death benefit when the insured person dies, or it could lead to the policy lapsing if the cash value gets depleted. However, in this case the policy has been overfunded, the cash value includes the amount of the laibilities and debts. The cash value is the collateral, once debt is paid, the money from the existing loan goes to the death benefit or face value. The client continues to earn the spread or the difference between the loan from the insurance company and the amount of compounded interest earned from the indexed amount earned.

6. Tax Implications: Loans against the cash value of a life insurance policy are generally not taxable as income. This is one of the key tax advantages. However, if the policy lapses or is surrendered with a loan outstanding, there could be tax consequences.

Benefits:
1. Tax-Deferred Growth: Cash value grows tax-deferred.

2. Tax-Free Loan: Borrowing against the policy is usually tax-free.

3. No Loan Requirement: Unlike a traditional loan, there's no requirement to repay unless you want to maintain the full death benefit. Again here the liabilities become collateral.

Why It's Not Used More:
1. Complexity: It's a complex strategy that requires careful planning and understanding. It requires long-term financial commitment and discipline.
2. Costs: Permanent life insurance policies can be expensive compared to term life insurance. But because of changes to IRS codes 7702 and 101a the price is much less expensive.
3. Risks: If not managed properly, the policy could lapse or become a MEC, leading to adverse tax consequences. However now the policy can be overfunded using liabilities.
4. Not Suitable for Everyone: Before changes to the IRS codes 7702 and 101a, this strategy was more beneficial for individuals in higher tax brackets or those with a long-term horizon.

This overview provides a basic understanding, but it's a nuanced topic, and individual circumstances can significantly affect the appropriateness and effectiveness of such a strategy. It's a complex strategy that requires careful planning and ongoing management. The potential benefits must be weighed against the costs and risks involved.

Watch Video
Hybrid Mortgage Arbitrage

Building Wealth & Protecting Love Ones!

Indexed universal life (IUL) insurance policies can help you to build wealth while leaving behind a death benefit for your loved ones. These policies put a portion of the policyholder's premium payments toward annual renewable term life insurance, with the remainder added to the cash value of the policy after insurance costs are deducted. On a monthly or annual basis, the cash value is credited with interest based on increases in an equity index.

Summary Of The Solution

1. Accelerated Debt Payment: The technology acts like a GPS, directing funds in the most efficient way to pay off debts earlier than the standard term. It can reduce the interest paid and help users to become debt-free more quickly. This is akin to the snowball or avalanche methods of paying off debt, but it's driven by AI and algorithms. The technology integrates with the IUL, enhancing the policy's characteristics based on the changes of the IRS codes 7702 and 101a in the Cares Act 2020.

2. Using Index Universal Life Insurance (IUL) for Banking Purposes: This is an advanced financial strategy that goes much further than the "Infinite Banking Concept" or "Bank on Yourself." With an IUL, there's potential to earn tax free interest based on index market performance without the risk of losing principal. Furthermore, policyholders can borrow against their IUL cash value, effectively "banking" with their policy.

The idea is that instead of paying interest to a bank, lender or even the life insurance company, they're not paying back the loan, they are paying off debt in record time, overfunding the IUL with the policy owners liabilities and theoretically earning the interest on themselves.

3. Tax Advantages: One of the key benefits of an IUL is its tax-advantaged growth. Earnings within this policy are not taxable. Furthermore, loans against the policy typically aren't considered taxable income.

Watch Short Video?
A Different Solution

How Life Insurance Agents Get Paid?

We are life insurance agents. Life insurance agents typically make money through commissions, bonuses, and sometimes salaries. Here's a breakdown of these income sources:

1. Commissions: This is the primary way life insurance agents earn money. Commissions are a percentage of the premium paid by the policyholder. The commission rate varies based on the type of policy (term life, whole life, universal life, etc.) and the insurance company's policies. For example, an agent might earn a high commission on the first year's premium, often ranging from 40% to 100% of that premium, and then a smaller commission in subsequent years for as long as the policy is in force.

2. Hybrid Retirement Arbitrage Commission: Because this policy is similar to that of a BOLI policy, the agent is paid the initial commission over 6 years. Not in advance, as the policy allows the owner to borrow against the cash value, has a higher MEC and has no surrender charge. Commissions are larger in subsequent years. The client must build wealth while continuing to use the policy, for the agent to get paid.

3. Renewal Commissions: For some policies, agents continue to receive a commission in the years following the initial sale, as long as the policyholder keeps paying the premiums. These renewal commissions are usually a smaller percentage than the initial commission.

4. Bonuses: Many insurance companies offer bonuses to agents for selling a certain number of policies or reaching certain sales targets. These bonuses can be a significant part of an agent's income, especially for those who are particularly successful in selling policies.

5. Salaries: Some agents, particularly those who work directly for an insurance company as opposed to independent agents, may receive a base salary in addition to commissions and bonuses. The balance between salary and commission varies widely among companies and individual positions.

6. Fees for Financial Planning Services: Some life insurance agents are also licensed financial planners and may charge fees for providing financial planning services.

7. Overrides: If an agent has a managerial role and oversees other agents, they may earn override commissions based on the sales of the agents they manage.

The structure of an agent's compensation can be complex and varies widely across the industry. It's also influenced by factors like the agent's experience, the types of policies they sell, and their employer's policies.

Our pay is based on your satisfaction, we truly get paid by making you happy and developing a relationship with you. You become our lifelong client.

How Life Insurance Works?

Theses terms pertain primarily to life insurance policies, especially those that build cash value, such as whole life, universal life, and variable life insurance policies. Here's a breakdown of each term:

1. Cash Value vs. Face Value of an Insurance Policy:

a. Cash Value: This is a component of certain life insurance policies. It represents a savings or investment portion that accumulates over time, based on the premiums you pay. The cash value grows tax-deferred and can be used in various ways during the policyholder's lifetime.

b. Face Value: This is the death benefit or the amount that will be paid to the beneficiaries upon the death of the insured. It's essentially the coverage amount you select when you purchase the policy.

2. Uses of Cash Value:

a. Borrow Against It: You can take out a loan against the cash value of your policy, typically at a lower interest rate than conventional loans. However, unpaid loans and interest may reduce the death benefit.

b. Withdrawals: Some policies allow you to withdraw a portion of the cash value. This might reduce the death benefit.

c. Premium Payments: Cash value can sometimes be used to pay premiums, ensuring the policy remains in force even if you can't make out-of-pocket payments.

d. Surrender Value: If you surrender the policy, you receive the current cash value, minus any surrender charges.

How Life Insurance Works? - Part 2

1. Face Value Working:

The face value is paid out to beneficiaries tax-free upon the death of the insured. It's not typically affected by the growth of the cash value unless the policyholder makes specific changes to the policy.

2. Overfunding:

Overfunding a life insurance policy means paying more into the policy than the minimum required premium. This accelerates the growth of the cash value. However, there are limits (like the MEC limit in the U.S.) to prevent the policy from being classified as a Modified Endowment Contract, which can have adverse tax consequences. However, because of the changes in the IRS codes 7702 and 101a, the MEC limits are higher, without premiums payments rising to match the MEC.

3. No Surrender Charge:

A surrender charge is a fee charged if a policy is surrendered or canceled before a certain period. A policy with no surrender charge means you can surrender the policy and take the cash value without any penalty. This feature might come with higher premiums or other trade-offs.

4. Living Benefits:

Living benefits in a life insurance policy allow the insured to access a portion of the death benefit under certain conditions while they are still alive. These are typically triggered by terminal illness, chronic illness, or the need for long-term care. It's a way to address financial needs that arise due to severe health issues.

Each policy has its own terms and conditions, and it's crucial to understand them thoroughly before purchasing or making changes to your life insurance coverage. Always consult with a qualified insurance professional to get advice tailored to your specific needs and circumstances.

Watch Video
More About Our Life Insurance

How Life Insurance Works? - Part 3

A target premium in a whole life insurance policy refers to a specific payment amount recommended by the insurance company. This amount is not the minimum required to keep the policy in force but is suggested to ensure that the policy achieves certain financial objectives, like providing a mix of life insurance protection and cash value accumulation.

Here's how it generally works:

1. Minimum Premium: This is the lowest amount you must pay to keep the policy active and maintain the death benefit. Paying only the minimum premium might slow the growth of the policy's cash value.

2. Target Premium: The target premium is higher than the minimum premium. It is set at a level that, if paid, helps the policy to perform as projected, typically allowing for more robust cash value growth and potential dividends (if it's a participating policy). It's a guideline rather than a requirement.

3. Cash Value Accumulation: By paying the target premium, the policy's cash value is likely to grow more quickly. This cash value can be used in various ways, such as borrowing against it, or it can simply serve as a financial cushion.

4. Flexibility: One of the advantages of whole life insurance is its flexibility in premium payments. You can usually choose to pay the minimum, the target, or an amount in between. Some policies even allow you to pay more than the target premium, further increasing the policy's cash value.

5. Policy Performance: Paying the target premium can also ensure that the policy performs as illustrated at the time of purchase, assuming non-guaranteed elements like dividends remain constant.

6. Non-Guaranteed Elements: It's important to remember that any projections made when the policy is purchased, especially regarding cash value growth and dividends, are based on current assumptions and are not guaranteed.

In summary, while the target premium is not the minimum required payment, paying it can help ensure that the policy achieves its intended balance of insurance protection and financial growth. Policyholders should regularly review their policies and discuss with their financial advisors to align their payments with their changing financial goals and needs.

Watch Video
Difference From Anything Else

How Life Insurance Works - Part 4 (BOLI)

1. $24,037,000,000   Bank of America
2. $19,369,000,000   Wells Fargo Bank
3. $12,115,000,000   JPMorgan Chase Bank
4. $10,572,902,000   PNC Bank
5. $7,515,000,000   Truist Bank
6. $6,113,011,000   U.S. Bank
7. $5,299,000,000   Citibank
8. $4,571,000,000   The Bank of New York Mellon
9. $4,136,211,000   KeyBank
10. $3,604,000,000   State Street Bank & Trust
11. $3,416,000,000   Regions Bank
12. $3,339,718,000   First Republic Bank
13. $3,222,477,000   BMO Harris Bank
14. $3,161,043,000   Citizens Bank
15. $2,691,240,000   The Huntington National
16. $2,090,000,000   Fifth Third Bank
17. $1,968,253,000   Santander Bank, N.A.
18. $1,957,241,000   Capital One
19. $1,793,313,000   TD Bank
20. $1,575,890,000   Flagstar Bank
21. $1,411,000,000   Comerica Bank
22. $1,242,648,000   Webster Bank
23. $1,099,229,000   Synovus Bank
24. $1,017,250,000   First Horizon Bank
25. $984,881,000   SouthState Bank

Learn More
BOLI & COLI

The above is a ranking is the top 25 banks out of over 3,000 in the United States in terms of "Life Insurance Assets". This comparison is based on data reported on 2023-09-30. Published by US Bank.

Can Anyone Bank Like A Bank?

Bank Like a Bank is different from any other banking solution in the market today. Bank Like a Bank is not only different from Infinite Banking, Be Your Own Bank, Become Your Own Bank, Bank On Yourself or Family Banking, but the goal of these strategies is not the same.

One is about using life insurance as a bank to finance consumer goods, banking like a bank is about canceling interest by paying debt early, overfunding the policy, using that debt to build income and generational wealth.

Unlike BYOB or Infinite Banking, with banking like a bank, people can borrow against their debt, earn interest on that debt, during & after the debt is paid, without tax & without paying back the loan. Banking Like a Bank was only possible after the IRS codes 7702 & 101a passed by congress changed in the Cares Act 2020.

Bank Like a Bank was researched, developed and implemented by Ron Harris, the CEO of Financial literacy Group, in March of 2021 and the Bank Like a Bank app was released in April, 2023.

Bank like a Bank is a unique combination of GPS debt technology & a special kind of liquid index universal life insurance. This solution is too new for most agents or advisors to offer or talk about, and with all the noise out there about life insurance it is too new even for influencers. So as a Certified Financial Planner (CFP) not knowing about this means, they really don't know about all solutions that are available.

The goal of Banking like a Bank is not to use a whole life insurance policy and your personal bank, the goal is to strategically optimize your debt pay off using technology, eliminating up to 75% of the interest, while paying off your debt or mortgage in less than 5 to 7 years, without changing you budget or lifestyle.

Not any or every whole life policy will work here, the strategy only works with a Bank Owned Life Insurance (BOLI) type of policy or Private Owned Life Insurance (POLI) has no surrender charges, no caps & no fees.

Regardless of what advisors say, equity is real money, with amortization a 6% APR on a mortgage, equals more interest than the cost of the house itself and losing money in the stock market happens everyday.

Bank like a Bank is a type of Hybrid Arbitrage that deals with any kind of debt including credit cards, residential & commercial mortgages, auto, equity, personal, student, equipment & business loans. Rather than using a HELOC or a Savings Account as an offset account, using the Index Universal Life Insurance policy allows the user to make tax free income on their early mortgage or debt pay off.

The money a person uses to pay their debt never leaves the IUL, they earn tax free interest on their liabilities for the rest of their lives. Policy holders have little or no risk, because they are receiving the return from the indices that would normally go to the life insurance company. Homeowners or debtors make the interest on their past and future loans & never pay them back. Bank like a bank, actually equalizes the financial playing field & closes the wealth gap forever.

Effect Of Adding A No Fee Annuity?

This description outlines a complex financial strategy involving several products: a single premium index annuity, a no capped index universal life (IUL) insurance policy, and various retirement accounts (TSA, 401K, IRA, pension). Here's a breakdown and analysis of the strategy:

1. Single Premium Index Annuity (SPIA):
   a. Features: No fees, annual accrual, protection against loss of premium, and a step-up basis that doubles the income producing asset.

   b. Rollover from Retirement Accounts: Rolling over a lump sum from a TSA, 401K, IRA, or pension into the SPIA before or at age 59 1/2. It's crucial to note that rollovers from these accounts might have tax implications, especially if they're pre-tax accounts, however there is no penalty when rolling over into an annuity. Rolling over before 59 1/2 usually incurs no penalty if done correctly, but income taxes on the rollover amount might still apply.

   c. Withdrawal Strategy: Withdraw 10% annually for the first 10 years, then switch to a guaranteed lifetime income stream. This approach must align with the specific rules of the annuity contract, as some annuities might have different terms for withdrawals and income.

2. Index Universal Life Insurance (IUL) Policy:
    a. Features: No cap on returns and no surrender charges, resembling a Bank-Owned Life Insurance (BOLI) style.
    b. Funding with Annuity Payments: The idea is to funnel both the 10% withdrawals from the SPIA and later the guaranteed income into the IUL policy.
    c. Borrowing Strategy: Borrow against the IUL policy, presumably at a lower interest rate than the earnings rate on the policy, thus enabling continuous growth of the policy's value while accessing cash.

3. Tax Strategy:
    The goal be to use the IUL policy to offset taxes paid on the non-qualified money originally rolled into the SPIA. This is based on the assumption that the growth within the IUL is tax-deferred and loans from IUL are tax-free.

4. Analysis and Considerations:

a. Complexity and Suitability: This strategy is complex and might not be suitable for all investors. It requires careful management and an understanding of the specific products involved.

b. Tax Implications: The tax treatment of such strategies can be complex and may vary depending on individual circumstances and changes in tax laws.

1. Product-Specific Rules: Each financial product (SPIA, IUL) has its own set of rules and limitations, which must be thoroughly understood.
2. Interest Rate Risks: The strategy assumes favorable borrowing rates and performance of the IUL, which may vary.
3. Long-Term Viability: Economic conditions, personal circumstances, and policy changes can impact the long-term viability of this strategy.
4. Professional Advice: It's crucial to seek advice from a financial advisor, tax professional, or attorney to understand the full implications and suitability of this strategy for your specific situation.

Remember, strategies involving annuities, life insurance products, and retirement accounts can be quite complex and are highly dependent on individual circumstances, as well as the specific terms of the products involved.

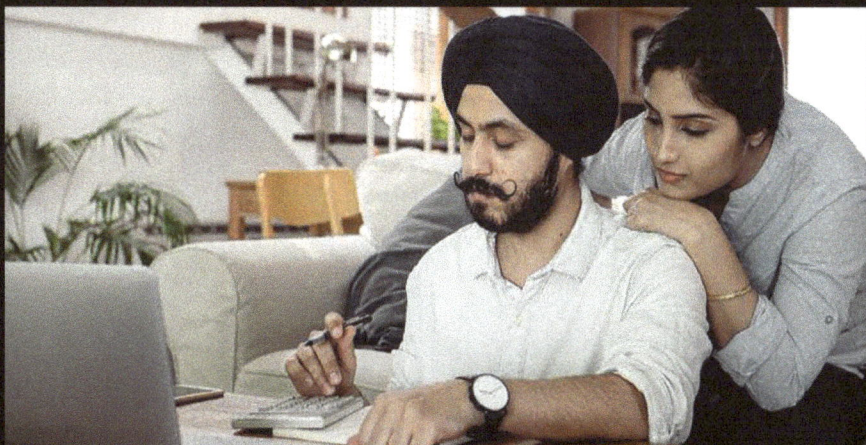

Alternative Research - March 2021

1. Become Financially Literate.

Online financial literacy course that equips individuals and families with the knowledge and skills to be able to make sound financial decisions that will help us manage money more effectively. It includes the understanding of how money works, how money is made, spent, and saved as well as how to manage debt. People with appropriate financial literacy generally are better at making financial decisions and how to manage money.

2. Bookkeeping & Debt Mapping.

Bookkeeping software, the recording, on a regular basis, of a company's financial transactions. Software that tracks all information on its books to make key operating, investing, and financing decisions. Being aware of your current financial position, as well as the transactions that occur within your budget.

3. Manage Cash Flow.

Cash flow management is tracking and controlling how much money comes in and out of a business in order to accurately forecast cash flow needs. It's the day-to-day process of monitoring, analyzing, and optimizing the net amount of cash receipts—minus the expenses.

4. Eliminate a % of Current & Past Debt - Cancel a % of Current & Past Interest.

5. Eliminate a % of Future Debt - Cancel a % of Future Interest

Debt Manager and our go debt free program uses sophisticated technology that serves as a financial GPS to direct the user to pay off their 30 year mortgage in as little as 5-7 years, with no change to your budget.

Consumers who use this smart debt elimination tool will save up to 70% of the interest on their 1st and/or 2nd mortgage, without changing budget. Our go debt free solution shows the user the exact date they will be debt free and its debt reduction results are proven.

The technology works on all kinds of debt; credit cards, residential and commercial mortgages, auto, equity, personal, student, equipment and business loans. The technology can manage multiple mortgages and all personal and/or business debt simultaneously, it can also be securely connected to most bank accounts.

6. Open Your Own Bank (Liquid, Uncapped IUL).

Using Index Universal Life Insurance (IUL) for Banking Purposes: This is an advanced financial strategy that goes much further than the "Infinite Banking Concept" or "Bank on Yourself." With an IUL, there's potential to earn tax free interest based on index market performance without the risk of losing principal. Furthermore, policyholders can borrow against their IUL cash value, effectively "banking" with their policy. The idea is that instead of paying interest to a bank, lender or even the life insurance company, they're not paying back the loan, they are paying off debt in record time, overfunding the IUL with the policy owners liabilities and theoretically earning the interest on themselves.

7. Turn Liabilities into Income and Wealth.

8. Accelerated Debt Payment: The technology acts like a GPS, directing funds in the most efficient way to pay off debts earlier than the standard term. It can reduce the interest paid and help users to become debt-free more quickly. This is akin to the snowball or avalanche methods of paying off debt, but it's driven by AI and algorithms. The technology integrates with the IUL, enhancing the policy's characteristics based on the changes of the IRS codes 7702 and 101a in the Cares Act 2020.

Learn More
About Annuities

9. Create an Estate or Death Benefit.

Indexed universal life (IUL) insurance policies can help you to build wealth while leaving behind a death benefit for your loved ones. These policies put a portion of the policyholder's premium payments toward annual renewable term life insurance, with the remainder added to the cash value of the policy after fees are deducted. On a monthly or annual basis, the cash value is credited with interest based on increases in an equity index.

10. Implement Mortgage Strategy.

Basically, it means sending extra mortgage payments to your lender to pay down your loan principal faster. Not only does it get you out of debt quicker, but it'll also help you save money by reducing interest charges and the total amount of interest you'll pay.

11. Develop a School Tuition Plan.

Starting to take steps to save and invest earlier allows parents to take advantage of more years of potential growth through compound earnings over time, especially when using a tax-advantaged investing vehicle such as 529 plans or an IUL. Parents know that using savings is vastly less expensive than incurring debt, and 65% are actively saving for their children's college costs. We are encouraged to see that parents are avidly saving and are motivated to avoid taking on debt for themselves and their children.

12. Implement Student Loan Strategy.

Accelerated Debt Payment: The technology acts like a GPS, directing funds in the most efficient way to pay off debts earlier than the standard term. It can reduce the interest paid and help users to become debt-free more quickly. This is akin to the snowball or avalanche methods of paying off debt, but it's driven by AI and algorithms. The technology integrates with the IUL, enhancing the policy's characteristics based on the changes of the IRS codes 7702 and 101a in the Cares Act 2020.

13. Borrow Against Your Debt or Liabilities.

Using Index Universal Life Insurance (IUL) for Banking Purposes: This is an advanced financial strategy that goes much further than the "Infinite Banking Concept" or "Bank on Yourself." With an IUL, there's potential to earn tax free interest based on index market performance without the risk of losing principal. Furthermore, policyholders can borrow against their IUL cash value, effectively "banking" with their policy. The idea is that instead of paying interest to a bank, lender or even the life insurance company, they're not paying back the loan, they are paying off debt in record time, overfunding the IUL with the policy owners liabilities and theoretically earning the interest on themselves.

14. Open a Single Payment No Fee Indexed Annuity SPIA.

PROTECT your principal, GROW your savings securely, GET INCOME — predictable and guaranteed for life Make your income last a lifetime. You have saved diligently for your retirement — but can you make your savings last for the rest of your life? Guaranteed Lifetime Income Rider (GLIR) can help your savings become retirement income that you can never outlive, while you still retain access to the remaining cash value. When the GLIR benefit is activated, you are guaranteed a predictable income stream for the rest of your life!

59 and ½ Rollover 401K, IRA or Retirement Account into Indexed Annuity - Create Increased Wealth & Build a 2nd Death Benefit. The lifetime income you receive is determined by the amount in the Benefit Calculation Base, which is not a value that can be withdrawn.

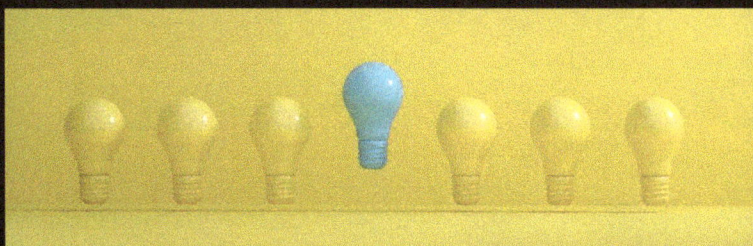

15. Double Your Income Producing Asset.

Maximize Funds & Equity for Retirement. Double Your Income Producing Asset, Take Withdrawals form the Rollover Funds in the first 10 Years.

Fixed-indexed annuities are a hybrid of fixed and variable annuities, our annuity has no fees and it accredits annually. They pay an interest rate that is tied to the performance of your chosen market index, but they also have a fixed minimum interest rate usually 0%. That means you'll never lose any of your initial premium, but you might not gain anything either.

You can withdraw money from an annuity without incurring a surrender charge if your provider allows and if you meet specific criteria. For example, there may be exceptions to the surrender charge in your contract. In this case you are allowed to take out 10% each year.

PROTECT your principal, GROW your savings securely, GET INCOME — predictable and guaranteed

16. Earn Back Tax Paid & Additional Interest From Your Nest Egg.

Put withdrawals in your bank, loan them to yourself to earn interest on principal & tax. By putting your withdrawn funds including the taxes owed into the Index Universal Life insurance policy allows the policy owner to earn deferred interest on the entire amount of the withdrawals.

The cash value in an IUL policy can be accessed via policy loans or withdrawals. Policy loans are generally not taxable, as they are considered debts, not distributions. However, if the policy lapses or is surrendered with a loan outstanding, the loan balance becomes taxable.

17. Turn On the Annuity's Guaranteed Annual Distribution at 68 to 70 Years of Age.

An annuity is a contract between you and an insurance company where you make one or more contributions and then you can elect to take withdrawals or guaranteed annuity payments after you retire. Annuities are designed to provide a stream of income that can last for the rest of your life, which can be helpful if you're worried about outliving your savings.

In this way, annuities are often used to supplement other sources of retirement income, such as monthly Social Security payments or a pension.

18. Put Each Distribution in Your Bank, Loan It to Yourself Earn Interest on Both Principal and Tax

By putting your distributed funds or guaranteed annual payments including the taxes owed into the Index Universal Life insurance policy allows the policy owner to earn deferred interest on the entire amount of the distributions. Here you are duplicating what you did with withdrawals in the first 10 years.

19. Tax Implications from Rollover Money - 401Ks to Annuities.

It's important to remember that annuities are taxed as ordinary income, so you may owe taxes on your withdrawals. That means any gains you earn from your annuity fall into your marginal tax bracket and could push you into the next tax bracket.

20, Pay Taxes From Money Loaned to You By Your Bank

Pay the federal taxes owed on the qualified distributed funds that were originally moved from the 401K to the Annuity then to the IUL and loaned to the policyowner. Money to the policyowner loaned from the IUL policy is not taxable.

What is the Ideal Annuity?

Learn More About Annuities

Ultimate Retirement Solution!

This retirement scenario involves a combination of financial strategies that aim to optimize personal finances in several ways: accelerated debt repayment, leveraging life insurance as a financial instrument, and potentially earning interest on personal loans. Let's break down the implications and potential outcomes of each aspect:

1. Early Debt Payoff Technology and Interest Elimination: Paying off debt early, especially high-interest debt like credit cards or certain types of loans, can save a significant amount of money in interest. Tools or strategies that help individuals pay off their debts faster (like debt snowball or avalanche methods) can lead to increased savings and a quicker path to financial freedom.

2. Using Indexed Universal Life Insurance as a Personal Bank: This strategy involves using an indexed universal life insurance policy as a savings and loan vehicle. The policy accumulates cash value by overfunding it with your liabilities, which can be borrowed against.

This strategy has its pros and cons:
 Pros: Tax benefits (life insurance proceeds are often tax-free), potential for higher returns (linked to a stock index), and flexibility in premium payments.

 Cons: It requires substantial understanding and management, and there are fees and potential risks associated with the investment component.

Book Us
Schedule Appointment

POOR
AVERAGE
GOOD
EXCELLENT

3. Paying Off a 30-Year Mortgage in 5 Years: This is an ambitious goal and would typically require significantly higher payments towards the principal, without a drastic change in lifestyle or budget, or a substantial increase in income. Without these changes, achieving such a goal might be seem unrealistic for most people. But with AI driven technology it can be done with discretionary income.

4. Duplicating BOLI (Bank-Owned Life Insurance) Strategies: BOLI is a practice where banks purchase life insurance policies for their employees and are the beneficiaries of the policies. This practice is mainly used for tax benefits and additional income through the policy's cash value growth. While individuals can't exactly duplicate BOLI, because of IRS code changes 7702 & 101a, during the cares act 2020, they can use similar concepts with personal life insurance policies.

5. Earning Interest on Own Loans: This typically refers to the cash value in a life insurance policy that you can borrow against. While you're paying interest on these loans, you're also potentially earning interest on the cash value, which can sometimes offset the cost of borrowing.

6. Moving from Recourse to Non-Recourse Loans: This would imply a shift in the type of debt one holds. A non-recourse loan is secured by collateral (usually real estate), and the lender can't pursue anything other than the collateral if the borrower defaults. This can be beneficial in protecting personal assets.

7. Doubling the Income Producing Asset: This is likely referring to the growth of an investment or savings vehicle, like life insurance or a annuity. Achieving this depends on the rate of return and the time frame involved.

8. Best Tax Advantages: Utilizing tax-advantaged accounts and strategies is crucial in financial planning. This can include retirement accounts, certain types of life insurance, health savings accounts, annuities, and more.

9. Without Changing Budget or Lifestyle: This is the most challenging aspect. Significant financial changes like paying off a mortgage early or substantially growing savings usually require either an increase in income, a decrease in expenses, or a combination of both., but in this case it requires neither.

Overall Impact: If individuals and families could effectively implement these strategies without altering their budget or lifestyle, it could lead to faster accumulation of wealth, reduced financial stress, and potentially earlier financial independence. However, it's important to note that these strategies require careful planning, disciplined financial management, and often, a good understanding of financial products and markets. As with any financial strategy, there are risks involved, and it's advisable to consult with a financial educator to understand these strategies' suitability for individual financial situations.

Download Now!
Intake Sheet

Who is Underwriting This Solution?

1. History:

Founded in 1848: National Life Group was established in Montpelier, Vermont. It is one of the oldest insurance companies in the United States.

a. Early Growth: The company grew steadily through the 19th and 20th centuries, expanding its product offerings and geographical footprint.

b. Expansion and Diversification: Over the years, National Life Group has diversified its services, including life insurance, annuities, mutual funds, and other financial products.

2. Key Stats and Facts:

National Life Group, as of our last update in December 2023, is a diversified financial services company that offers a variety of life insurance, annuity, and investment products. Here are key aspects of the company:

a. Headquarters: National Life Group is headquartered in Montpelier, Vermont.

b. Financial Strength: The company is known for its financial stability. It typically receives strong ratings from insurance rating agencies.

c. Product Range: Its product offerings include life insurance, annuities, retirement plans, and investment products.

d. National Life Insurance Company: This is the flagship company of National Life Group, primarily focused on life insurance products.

e. Structure: The organization operates through its key subsidiaries, including National Life Insurance Company, Life Insurance Company of the Southwest, Sentinel Investments, and Equity Services, Inc.

f. Ownership: National Life Group is a mutual company, meaning it is owned by its policyholders rather than public shareholders. This can influence its business strategies, often focusing more on long-term stability and benefits for policyholders rather than short-term profits.

g. Position Among Peers: National Life Group is not one of the largest insurers in the U.S. when compared to giants like MetLife, New York Life, or Northwestern Mutual. However, it has carved out a reputation for stability and reliability in its market segment.

h. Community and Social Responsibility: The company has a history of community involvement and corporate social responsibility. They have initiatives focused on education, economic development, and environmental sustainability.

3. Recent Developments:

a. Technological Advancements: Like many financial institutions, National Life Group has been investing in digital technologies to improve customer experience and operational efficiency.

b. Sustainability Initiatives: The company may have engaged in efforts to become more environmentally sustainable and socially responsible.

c. Market Performance: The recent performance in terms of business growth, market expansion, and financial stability should be verified from the latest reports and news.

4. Notable Achievements:

a. Longevity in the Market: National Life Group's survival and growth over more than a century is a significant achievement, reflecting its ability to adapt to changing market conditions.

b. Customer Loyalty: The company has historically been known for strong customer relationships and loyalty.

For the most current information, including the latest annual reports and news releases, visiting National Life Group's official website or looking at recent financial news sources would be advisable. Remember that the financial services industry is subject to rapid changes and regulatory developments, so the latest information is key for an accurate understanding of the company's current status.

Mutual Life vs. Public Life Insurance!

A mutual life insurance company and a public (or stock) life insurance company primarily differ in their ownership structures and how they distribute profits.

1. Ownership:

Mutual Life Insurance Company: These are owned by their policyholders. People who buy insurance policies from a mutual life insurance company are effectively its shareholders. This means that policyholders have certain rights, such as voting on the board of directors and other company decisions.

Stock Life Insurance Company: Public or stock life insurance company is owned by shareholders who have purchased the company's stock. These shareholders may or may not be policyholders. The primary goal of a stock company is to maximize shareholder value.

2. Profit Distribution:

Mutual Life Insurance Company: Since the policyholders are the owners, any profits (referred to as "surplus") are typically either reinvested into the company to improve its services or returned to the policyholders in the form of dividends or reduced future premiums.

Stock Life Insurance Company: Profits are mainly distributed to the shareholders in the form of dividends. The company may also reinvest profits back into the business.

3. Decision Making and Focus:

Mutual Life Insurance Company: The focus tends to be more on long-term stability and benefits for the policyholders. Decision-making is generally considered to be more conservative, prioritizing the interests of the policyholders.

Stock Life Insurance Company: There may be more emphasis on short-term financial performance since they need to meet the expectations of stock market investors. They might take more aggressive investment or business strategies.

How life Insurance Companies Make Money:

a. Premiums: The most obvious source of revenue is the premiums paid by policyholders. These premiums are calculated based on various risk factors to ensure that the company collects enough money to pay out claims and still profit.

b. Investment Income: Life insurance companies invest a large portion of the premiums they collect. They typically invest in a diverse portfolio that includes bonds, stocks, real estate, and other financial instruments. The returns from these investments are a significant source of income for these companies.

c. Underwriting Profits: This is the difference between the premiums collected and the money paid out in claims and other expenses. Efficient underwriting (assessing the risks and setting premiums accordingly) is crucial for profitability.

d. Service Fees and Other Income: Depending on their business model, life insurance companies may also earn money from service fees, policy renewal fees, and other financial services they offer.

The business models of mutual and stock life insurance companies influence how they balance these revenue streams and their overall strategies for profitability.

National Life Group is a mutual company, NLG is the number one seller of IUL poloicies is 2023. They are the only company that would allow us to offer the same kind of policy as the banks use BOLI, to middle class Americans.

Wealth Building Options - Global Real Estate

As of my last update in December 2023, investing in property remains a popular strategy for wealth building, and there are several locations around the world that have been highlighted as promising for real estate investment. However, it's important to remember that the real estate market can be dynamic and influenced by numerous factors, including economic conditions, political stability, and market trends. Here's a breakdown of your questions:

A. Best Places to Invest in Property in the World in 2023

1. Portugal: Known for its Golden Visa program, offering residency to property investors.

2. Germany: Particularly cities like Berlin and Frankfurt, known for their stable markets and growth potential.
3. United States: Areas like Austin, Texas, and Raleigh, North Carolina, are popular for their growing economies and population.
4. Spain: Especially in cities like Madrid and Barcelona and coastal areas.

5. Japan: Tokyo, for its stability and strong rental market.

B. Why Buying Property is a Good Wealth Building Move

1. Appreciation: Over time, property values generally increase.

2. Rental Income: It can generate a steady income stream.

3. Leverage: Real estate allows for the use of leverage (mortgages) to increase potential return.

4. Diversification: It's a tangible asset that diversifies your investment portfolio.

5. Tax Advantages: Depreciation, mortgage interest deductions, and other tax benefits.

Set An Appointment
Let Us Schedule a Tour?

Wealth Building Options - Global Real Estate 2

C. Should You Buy a Vacation Property?

Pros:

1. Personal Enjoyment: A place for holidays and creating memories.

2. Rental Income Potential: When not in use, it can be rented out.

3. Appreciation: Potential for value increase over time.

Cons:

1. Costs: Ongoing maintenance, property management, insurance, and taxes.

2. Market Risk: Vacation properties can be more sensitive to market fluctuations.

3. Limited Use: Depending on location, there might be seasonal limitations.

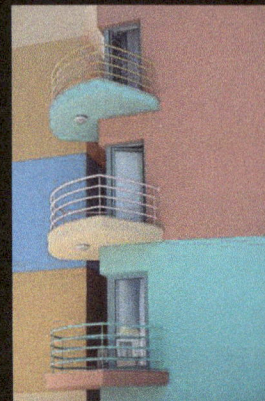

D. Is it Safe to Buy Real Estate in Other Countries?

Safety in buying real estate abroad depends on:

1. Legal Framework: Understanding property laws and rights in the country.

2. Political Stability: Countries with stable governments are generally safer.

3. Economic Conditions: Strong economies tend to have safer real estate markets.

4. Local Market Knowledge: Understanding local market dynamics is crucial.

E. Pros and Cons of Buying Real Estate in Other Countries

Pros:

1. Diversification: Geographic and economic diversification.

2. Potential High Returns: Emerging markets can offer high growth potential.

3. Lifestyle Benefits: Personal use and enjoyment, especially in desirable locations.

Cons:

1. Legal and Regulatory Risks: Different laws and processes.

2. Market Unfamiliarity: Less knowledge of the local market dynamics.

3. Currency Risk: Fluctuations in currency value can affect returns.

4. Management Challenges: Remote property management can be complex.

F. Final Thoughts

Always conduct thorough research and consider consulting with real estate professionals, financial advisors, and legal experts, especially when investing in foreign markets. Each investor's situation is unique, and what works for one may not be suitable for another.

We have representation in countries and areas listed, only.

Wealth Building Option - RE in La Paz, Mexico

La Paz, Mexico, has been gaining attention as a potential real estate investment location. Here are some points to consider if you're thinking about investing in property there, particularly for wealth building or as a vacation property:

A. Pros of Buying Real Estate in La Paz, Mexico:

1. Growing Popularity: La Paz has been emerging as a popular destination, particularly for those seeking a more authentic Mexican experience compared to more commercialized locales.
2. Affordability: Compared to other popular coastal destinations in Mexico and many parts of the US, La Paz offers relatively affordable real estate prices.
3. Natural Beauty and Lifestyle: With its beautiful beaches, rich marine life, and relaxed lifestyle, it offers an appealing environment for vacationers and retirees.
4. Tourism Growth: Increasing tourism can lead to higher demand for vacation rentals, potentially providing a good return on investment.
5. Expatriate Community: A growing community of expatriates can make it easier to adapt and find support networks.
6. Cultural and Recreational Opportunities: Rich in culture and outdoor activities, offering diverse experiences for residents and tourists alike.

B. Cons of Buying Real Estate in La Paz, Mexico:

1. Market Volatility: Real estate markets can be unpredictable, especially in tourist-centric areas.

2. Legal Complexities: Foreigners buying property in Mexico face certain legal requirements, which can be complex and require due diligence.

3. Property Management Needs: If you're not living there year-round, you'll need reliable property management for maintenance and rentals.

4. Natural Disasters: As a coastal region, it can be prone to hurricanes and other natural events, necessitating robust insurance.

5. Economic Fluctuations: Local economy can be dependent on tourism, which is subject to fluctuations.

6. Safety Concerns: While La Paz is generally considered safer than many other parts of Mexico, it's important to stay informed about safety issues.

Safety in Buying Real Estate:

C. Regarding safety in real estate transactions, it's crucial to:

Hire a reputable local attorney who understands Mexican property law, especially the regulations regarding foreign ownership in the "restricted zone" (within 50 km of the coast and 100 km of the border).
1. Understand the Fideicomiso Process: As a foreigner, you'll likely buy property through a fideicomiso (bank trust), which is a common and secure method for foreigners to hold property in these zones.
2. Title Insurance: Consider purchasing title insurance to protect against any legal discrepancies.

D. Should You Buy a Vacation Property in La Paz?

This decision depends on your personal and financial circumstances, including your investment goals, risk tolerance, and affinity for the lifestyle in La Paz. If the local culture, environment, and potential for investment align with your interests and goals, it could be a worthwhile consideration. However, it's important to undertake comprehensive research and seek professional advice tailored to your specific situation.

Set an Appointment
Let Us Book a Tour?

Learn How To Fish For Yourself!

1. Combination of Technology & Life Insurance

2. Pay Your Debt & Liabilities Off Early

3. Pay a 30 Year Mortgage in as Little as 5-7 Years

4. Eliminate Up To 75% of Your Interest

5. Turn Your Liabilities into Income & Wealth

6. Duplicate The Banks & Corporations (BOLI & COLI)

7. You Earn Interest On Your Own Loans

8. Move From Recourse to a Non-Recourse Position

9. Get The Best Tax Advantages Now & In The Future

10. Indexing Options No Caps, No Surrender Charges

11. Never Lose Principal, Zero Percent Floor

12. Double Income Producing Asset with No Fees

13. Use Global Real Estate as a Safe Haven For Your Money

14. No Change to Budget, Lifestyle or Cash Flow

15. No Refinance, Modification, Consolidation or Settlement

As Our Client, We Put You First!

We are dedicated to helping working class individuals, families and small business owners like you reach a comfortable retirement and build wealth. As financial educators we put our clients' interest first, but our solutions are structured with your well being in mind.

1. Commission Aligned With Your Interest

Our Commission schedule is transparent, our underwriter's pay structure is also transparent and our incentives are tied directly to your success. We do not make money if you are not happy, we don't make money when you are not making money, we only make money if you are generating or building wealth.

We don't make money on selling investment products with hidden fees, no trading, transaction, management, advisor, performance, broker or expense. No front-end fees or back-load fees, none of the common conflicts of interest that exist in much of the financial industry.

2. An Alternative Approach

Our alternative approach is to offer a personalized solution that is tailored to your unique situation: your financial goals, wants, needs, health, family and lifestyle. Our approach is an ongoing one, we work with you to understand changes in your life or financial situation, from your cash flow, through retirement and for the long term.

3. Unparalled Service

Your financial educator is here to serve you, not sell you. Your financial partner is well versed in your financial goals and will help you stay on track with your retirement plan. They will train, educate and call you to make sure you understand what you are doing and why you are doing it.

Our financial tools, educational resources, webinar, videos, content and client events also help you understand the challenging and often unpredictable markets.

4. Industry Experience

We have been working in the financial service industry since 1980. We meet and build cases the same way lawyers do. Our research of the IRS codes 7702 and 101a changes in the Cares Act 2020, demonstrates not our experience and our commitment to thinking outside of the box. Our underwriter was originally founded in 1848, they are a mutual company that serves working class Americans.

5. Do Your Due Diligence

Your friends will give you their opinion, maybe your spouse will tell you that this sounds too good to be true, you will now pay attention to the many influencers that have actually been online, before you learn about this option.

Advisors will tell you that they have a better way, other insurance agents will work to discourage you, telling you that this is not possible. But this solution is different from anything they have ever seen .

We want you to know that you are on the right path, this alternative solution is real, legal and not too good to be true. So we ask that you do your own due diligence so that you can make this important decision with all the knowledge you can gather.

What We Do?
Learn More

INTAKE SHEET

Date _____

'Your Current Debt Snapshot'

Name - _____   Phone# _____

Address - _____   Email - _____

_____

MORTGAGES

Lender Name	Mortgage Start Date	Mortgage Term	Monthly Payments*	Extra Principle Payments	Interest Rate	Escrow Payment	Mortgage Insurance Payment	Current Mortgage Balance	Original Purchase Price

__Including__ Principle, Interest, Escrow, PMI/Mortgage Insurance, etc.

LOANS

Account Name*	Loan Start Date	Loan Term	Monthly Payment	Extra Principle Payment	Interest Rate	Current Loan Balance	Original Loan Amount

Auto Loans, Student Loans, Personal Loans, Business Loans

REVOLVING CREDIT

Type of Credit*	Current Balance	Minimum Payment	Extra Principle Payment	Interest Rate	Credit Limit	Creditor Name

LOC - Line of Credit, Credit Card, HELOC - Home Equity Line of Credit

AVERAGE HOUSEHOLD NET INCOME

Income Source	Payment Frequency*	Average Net Income Per Paycheck

Monthly Expenses (All Bills--Food, Gas, Electric, Etc.) **Monthly Discretionary Income** (after Bills are Paid)	Life Ins. Co.		401k.Retirement Savings.403b
	Year Bot		Current Balance
	Face		Mo/Contrib
	Premium		Matched?
	Cash Value		Old 401k, 403b?
	Surr.Value		Old TSP, IRA, or?

Addt'l Info	State	Age	Date of Birth	Nicotine	Your Health	Any Medications
You						
Spouse						

RESET

112723jcp

THANK YOU

PROSPERITY

We Welcome Your Feedback

feel free to get in touch with us for any feedback or questions

Our Website
Visit Us

Watch Videos
Youtube Channel